The Tune of the Hickory Stick

Off to school — Mush!

Cover Concept:
Asian and David
MY FRIENDS' PLACE
17 Paris St.
Alliston, ON
L9R 1J3

Typeset and Printed by:
Stan Brown Printers Limited
Owen Sound, Ontario, Canada
1988

The Tune of the Hickory Stick

Tales Of A
Backwoods Teacher

Wilbur Leonard

ISBN: 0-9693560-0-5

Foreword

Every teacher's life is eventful. The trials and anxieties, particularly for the beginner, are indelibly impressed upon his memory. The succeeding events are actual happenings experienced in my first two years' teaching when I left Owen Sound for Northern Ontario in 1936, and these endurances are typical of those challenged by thousands of other teachers who begin their careers in undeveloped portions of Ontario.

Episodes

Episode I

Northward

My eyes welled up with tears as the train hustled away from the station platform at Owen Sound. Would I ever see my people again? I might be away one year, five years, ten years and even die in Northern Ontario. Six hundred miles of unknown vastness lay before me, and my mind was clouded with a hundred different kinds of destinations.

The next evening at six o'clock the train drew alongside a box car. I was marshalled off the passenger car only to realize that the station was Driftwood, my destination. The box car was the station. A chilling drizzle foreshadowed difficulties that night. A burly, Indian-faced man stepped up to me and inquired if I were the school teacher. He was the secretary of the Board. "Are you good for six miles?" he quizzed.

Just at this juncture the train began to pull away and my trustee asked me whether I had my baggage or not, and informed me that passengers are supposed to call at the baggage car for checked belongings. Between the two of us we dragged my weighty trunk to the ground with a thud. We left the trunk at the post office and there engaged two amateur taximen to take us as far as they could. They were French and looked to be brothers. We drove three miles along a gravelled road dented with water puddles. This was followed by a three-mile trek afoot. Half a mile in from the gravel was a low, flat, log house, with a family of curious children awaiting their new teacher. At their home I was to have supper. Half a mile from the log house was a curious teacher with his mind full of varied imaginings of what lay before him. I chucked the grinning taximen fifty cents, but would

7

have given thrice that amount if they could have taken us farther. As it was, the mucky clay glued to the road ahead, caught me by the ankles and my imaginings were rapidly giving place to realities. I had often read of the possibilities of the Great Clay Belt, but now I was experiencing them. I plunged through mire over my ankles, while my secretary was well geared with rubber boots and took to this river of muck like a turtle.

SECRETARY'S HOME

SECRETARY'S FAMILY
THE BALINTS

By the time we arrived at his place for supper, thick black night had sealed us in. A fine friendly family welcomed me. The children were well trained and polite. The oldest boy was fifteen and assumed the poise of his elders, joining in the conversation with the rest of us. He took after his father in physical stature and was to become a pupil of a city dude like me. However, I respected this boy. I liked him as soon as I set eyes upon his quiet gentlemanly ways. There was an older sister, and though large for her age, her gestures and movements were graceful, with no show. She took her mother's place quite capably in setting the table. Weeks later I learned that my application had been accepted because of my name and age which attracted this girl. Furthermore, I realized that my first personal appearance had given her a shock of resentment and disappointment.

The walls of the interior were white-washed with lime, the room being sparsely furnished with a table and a few home-hewn benches. The Hungarian goulash was delicious.

"I will take you to a lovely little spot to board. They are a nice couple and you will soon get to like them," commended my secretary as soon as supper was over. My imaginations began another whirl as we pushed into the inky sea of a cold September night with a little lantern whose glimmer penetrated the gloom only a few feet ahead. Again my ankles and shins were bathed in water and grime while I played follow-the-leader with my secretary for two and a half miles.

"This is the place," he gurgled the second time before I caught what he had said. As he opened the door, European peasantry displayed itself in a dozen ways. A sweet, chubby, smiling, kerchiefed little woman stood wringing her hands. These Hungarian people are wonderfully hospitable and after introductions were made the woman motioned to me to seat myself on a bench, and to remove my shoes and socks. My trousers were also plastered with mud, but she did not insist upon their removal. Without a word she hastily set a hot foot bath before me, standing there with her hands clasped and her face wreathed in innocent smiles, happy because she was doing a service. This foot-washing ceremony added an Eastern touch to the already-foreign atmosphere.

The lady's husband was short and stocky. He looked as if he had often used the recipe "laugh and grow fat." A good-natured lump he appeared to be.

Before my Hungarian secretary left to go home, we were ushered into a combined dining-room and bedroom. A case of home-brew was drawn from under one of the beds. Under the other bed were piled vegetables of all varieties. I did not partake of their brew as I had been strictly taught at home to revere the laws of temperance. There were two beds in the room and a table with benches fixed to the floor in the middle of the room. One bed was for me and I resolved

without question that the lady and her husband would oc-
cupy the other bed. I conjectured that theirs was the one
under which a whole cellar of brew was stored. What was to
be done about the undressing? Nothing. Disrobing proceeded as though we had known one another from infancy.

As the good-natured man puffed out the light in the coal-
oil lamp he chuckled something in Hungarian. I never heard
an English word in his house that night. What if I needed a
doctor? I must run two and a half miles to the secretary to
tell him. What if I were hungry? There were vegetables under
my bed. What if I were thirsty? Their bed?

MY FIRST BOARDING HOUSE

MA AND PA

Episode II

Friend and Foe

I awoke next morning from a pupa state of slumber to behold a steel-gray dawn. The air was keenly fresh but delicately spiced by squelched forest and grass fires. The misty drizzle had lifted to form a low ceiling of cold leaden clouds.

As I rose from my hay mattress, I discovered that my trousers were hanging neatly over the foot of the bed, laundered and pressed; and a pair of shoes carved and polished from the finest piece of East Indian ebony lay on the mat. I had caught the spirit of these people, but I could not reconcile myself to the foreign element. The speech barrier sent pangs of homesickness through me, and I made up my mind to remove this impediment by learning a few of the commonest Hungarian expressions as soon as possible.

Breakfast over, three French boys from a log dwelling across the road dropped in, primarily to size up their new teacher, but ostensibly on an errand for an equally nosy mother. Their faces were plastered with grins — not smiles. The tattletales had the biography of their past teacher down pat. They told how they had put him out of the school, how the teacher's sympathizers and the non sympathizers fought a pitched battle in the grassy school yard.

Later on in the day two teen-age girls dropped into the zoo. I restrained myself from stretching out my hand to collect a fee for the privilege of so closely scrutinizing their curio. In their own language, I discovered later, they politely nicknamed me "monkey." As I am not a supporter of Darwin's notions, I must confess that my own faith received quite a jolt.

THE FRENCH ELLEMENT BOYS

TEENAGE GIRLS

14

This was my day for "getting acquainted with the community," — an indispensable day according to the sermons preached to us by our Normal School masters. It was becoming quite evident that I did not have to leave the house to perform this duty. Passers-by, togged in peasant garb, gazed at the premises as though they were bewitched.

I called my guardians Ma and Pa. That afternoon Pa took me to the school. It was a frame building two years old, and the windows were arranged along the south side according to latest regulations. But the structure itself would have been a disgrace to Solomon. The interior was panelled with beaverboard which was warped out of position in several places. The blackboards were sections of painted beaverboard. My desk was a flimsy pantry table which rocked on its four legs. The little heater had rusted through in several spots, through which Pa and I could have had a game of peek-a-boo had we been in the mood. The floor was wet in two places, evidence of a faulty roof. Stonco, a Pole in the community, was contractor for the building of the school. He said he had experience in erecting buildings in warm and cold climates. It must have been an exceedingly hot summer when he built this African hut. My prophecy of a torturously cold school was to be realized that winter when ink froze on the pens of the pupils as they dipped them into their thawed bottles.

The outdoor toilets were exceptionally well built.

The woodshed was the skeletal remains of a log house, an ominous construction with the whole roof section tilted from one end to the other. A robin would find it drier to hop under a sieve during a rain storm than to flit into this shell of shambles.

The well was equipped with a good pump, but contained only surface water.

I had observed during the day that Ma and Pa knew an odd word of English, and when I arrived at the house following our inspection at the school, Ma said, "You mudda?" She looked into my eyes with her head tilted, and her

THE WOODSHED

countenance beaming with smiles. I returned a blank and puzzled stare. What did she mean? At repeated intervals that night the same question was put, and in the same manner. When, at last, it dawned on me that she was asking me about my mother, the delight of the little couple knew no bounds. They hugged one another and danced about the warped plank floor, while my emotions were stirred by these expressions of simple delight. My own sophistication repelled me from joining in the antics of the actors.

Tap! tap! and in walked another inquisitive visitor. Casting a side glance at me, the little six-year-old lassie hopped over to Ma and chattered in a bagpipe tone of voice. She held the floor for five minutes this way, pretending she did not notice me. However, she was a sweet little thing, with the flattened facial features of a Chinese baby, a wee mouth, wee fingers, a precocious and old-fashioned little lady. She certainly sounded as if she had a mastery of her own language, as she commanded the admiration and the attention of the three of us.

"And what is your name?" I interrupted.

"Helen Pal," she returned. "My home is over there," pointing out the window. "I have two brothers younger than myself."

"Who else lives there?"

"Mother and Father; but we have two horses and one cow."

"Where do they stay?"

"In the next room to us. I like them very much." Darwin gets another pat on the back.

As Helen marched with quick long strides through the low doorway, I followed her outside into the muddy yard and expressed my sentiments; "I'm glad you can speak English. Good-bye."

"Good-bye, teacher," and disappeared.

In the twilight dusk could be seen the shapeless forms of mud huts, identified more clearly by the lamp-lit windows. As the huts were built two to a lot and within a stone's throw of one another, the settlement, stretching three miles along the clay road, displayed a dazzle of myriad illuminations. This pretty sight was a balm for homesickness. Supper concluded the day with a tasty dish of horka, a sausage made of rice and ground pork liver. I spent a sleepless night, harassed with visions of my first day in school.

HELEN PAL — FRONT CENTRE

Episode III

Bozo

The autumn saw a November of heavy snowfalls. Wisps of smoke curled in soft spirals over the landscape, smoke that was escaping through small holes in the thick blanket of snow. Every year grass fires burn deep into the ground which holds live embers on into the winter.

By the last day of November Christmas concert practice was well under way. The unrisen sun, that morning, cast rosy hues on foamy clouds in the east. I arose early, for Pa had called me to shoot his pet pig. He would stick it if I shot it. He handed me a liberal handful of twenty-two calibre mushrooms, and I asked him if he had more if I should need them. He informed me that there were several boxes in his trunk.

"Open the stable door," he instructed me. "Bozo will come expecting his breakfast. Drop him in the doorway," he concluded in a confusion of English and Hungarian. I carried out these instructions, and to my surprise dropped him on the first shot. Ma and Pa came flying out of the house, one with the dish pan and the other flourishing the butcher knife. The sticking proceeded with Pa wielding the knife, Ma salvaging the blood, and me pumping a leg. I straightened myself up to behold an audience of school children on the road, rollicking in fits of laughter. We dragged Bozo to a coil of hay where he was singed in an inferno of heat. Pa could hardly wait till the blaze had completely died out to cut off a piece of ear to chew. My stomach allowed me only a bite of breakfast, and I hurried off to school.

19

BOZO'S STABLE
MA DRAWING WATER

When morning devotions were over, Helen Pal recited her story, "How the Pony was Shod." Spelling, reading, and arithmetic passed off as usual. I dismissed school at ten to twelve for I wanted to have a private talk with Frank Tindall regarding his work. Frank was a lovable boy of fourteen, and never hid the truth about anything.

"Haven't got any cigarettes on me, sir," as he turned his pockets inside out and even offered to remove his long leather boots for inspection.

"No, Frank. I know you haven't. But that is not why I want to see you." Frank was conscientious but very sensitive, and it would take the tact and understanding of a psychologist to deal correctly with the lad, and what a task for a greenhorn like me!

Dinner hour rolled by and the children assembled for a half hour singing practice. One can imagine the effect derived from a group of twenty-five children of ages six to seventeen, a mixture of Hungarians, Czecho-Slovaks, French and English, singing a three-part German carol.

Sixteen-year-old John Ellement looked unbearably bored, but I took no specific notice of him. Then, without warning, he left the room, even without asking permission. As this was not the custom I knew that something must be wrong, but went on with the singing to cause the least excitement possible amongst the pupils. After they were settled down to some seat work, I investigated John's case. I found him sitting on the door step, but he would neither talk to me nor look at me. John never acted this way before and I was becoming quite alarmed. He went back into the school to his seat and began to sob violently. I put a cup of water to his lips but he did not regard it. Suddenly he stiffened out in his seat, and it dawned on me that he was suffering from some form of epilepsy. I heaved him on to the floor and left him there till he revived an hour later.

FRANK TINDALL, BIG BILL BALINT, KEN BALINT

That was John's last day in school. He vowed he would never come again.

I was fagged out that night and ready to eat anything that was eatable. Bozo was occupying the dining-room table, so we ate in the kitchen. In my plate lay fifteen inches of blood sausage. I shall admit that the taste was much like that of liver; but I never understood clearly the power of the mind over the body until then. It was repulsive to my mind therefore my stomach revolted against it. Three inches of it, and no more, sufficed. Ma and Pa triumphantly ate blood sausage for thirty minutes, while I was settling mine with some orange marmalade and tea.

The next afternoon the inspector paid a visit to the school, and like most inexperienced teachers I tried to put on a special splurge, hoping to leave with him a good impression.

He said he had several books in his car out on the gravel, which were donated to our school library by the I.O.D.E. Two of the boys were only too glad to walk the three miles each way for the books. However, it was necessary to tell them to hurry.

Things were going splendidly until recess came and we were in the midst of a private conference when little Bob Tindall set up one of his unearthly howls. As he raced into the school, he stopped short in front of us, and put on a show of tonsils and crocodile tears. As I knew that all of this fuss was over a trivial matter, I said, "Run outside and play." He shut up like a clam and disappeared into the yard. No sooner had we resumed talking when the water monitor tripped on the threshold with his pail of water and a tidal wave swept toward the front of the room. A few quick side-steps saved the inspector and me from getting drowned.

As the inspector was leaving he advised me not to remain here for more than two years. He informed me that Kapuskasing was looking for a teacher. In the spring I took a train trip to apply for the job. The vacancy was already filled. Well do I remember the occasion. Kapuskasing is a company town, that is, the houses are constructed by the Abitibi Company and rented. The core of industry is the pulp mill. Thousands of cords of four-foot wood look like matches from a distance. The town is laid out in two circles. One circle of residences overlooks the river, and the other is a complete circle of stores. Kapuskasing Inn is a miniature Royal York Hotel and faces the river. Two dollars a night and seventy-five cents a breakfast took me beyond my pocket-book. So I searched the town for a lodging within my means. King Edward Hotel asked for thirty-five cents for the night. That was the place for me. The proprietor led me up a squeaky staircase, through a hall of smoky walls, and into a bedroom with warped floors and a coating of sand and dust which ground under my shoes. As the proprietor left, I attempted to close the door, but the absence of a knob and the warped condition of the floor made this impossible. I jumped on the bed to undress, but found myself marooned when I wanted to loosen the electric light bulb, as there was no switch. So I slipped on my oxfords and waded over to the light through the sand. The night passed uncomfortably, but I did not know why until next morning when I discovered an army of bed bugs under my pillow and in the sheets. Imagine the humiliation of King Edward if he could know that this hotel was named after him.

When the inspector left, I was worked up to such a pitch of excitement that I mercilessly grabbed a boy by the collar and shook him. While he was donning his coat he was grinning at something out of the window — a major offence at that moment, but nothing worth bothering about had I been in a calm frame of mind.

Thanks to Bozo that night! I enjoyed a hearty meal of rice sausage.

Episode IV

Excuse Me

Whether deficating or urinating, Bozo, the pig, had his privacy, but not so with me. I soon discovered that performing these necessary duties was as public and open as eating at the table.

The backhouse had three closed sides. The fourth side was open and exposed to the road. At home in Owen Sound I would sometimes take a book or a newspaper to the bathroom to read while I was sitting on the throne. I did not need to do this at Ma's place. I was entertained by watching the pedestrian traffic on the road. In turn they had a full view of me too, but it was no big thing. They would not stare at me out of curiosity, just as one would not stare at you while you were eating your dinner. This openness was part of the mores of European peasantry.

I was only in the settlement a few days when I discovered that there was no chamber pot under the bed to use in the middle of the night. One had to go outside if you wanted to empty the bladder. Even in the winter at 40° below zero, there was no getting away with it, you had to go outside. Before you were finished the draining process man's most precious commodity was starting to turn into a fleshy icicle.

The snowbank outside the door was polka-dotted with yellow stains. You would think it was a gathering place for the neighborhood dogs. Even Ma exposed her bare facts to the elements.

To have a bath at home we would use cistern water heated in a boiler on the cookstove. In this manure plastered hut we used rainwater in the summer and melted snow in the winter.

Our bathtub was the bottom half of a barrel. Bathing proceeded in full view of everybody.

I got more attention shaving with my safety razor, because Pa had one of those straight razors, a bloody weapon that made me shudder just to look at it. To this day I never allow a barber to come near me with his razor.

Episode V

Poppy

"Tanito! Tanito!" were the first words I heard one Saturday morning in September, and I struggled to arouse myself from a sound sleep. I opened my eyes to behold Ma's glaring down into mine. She was in a state of hyper excitement with hands circling and waving to form a sign language to which I was now accustomed. I nodded my head. There was a visitor in the kitchen waiting to see me. The first half of the dressing procedure was a blank. Sleep clung to me like the tentacles of a devil fish, as I grabbed for articles of clothing with my eyes shut.

In the kitchen was a little man of about thirty-five wearing a white shirt, white pants and a sombrero-shaped hat. He was slight in stature and deeply studying a picture magazine. As I entered the kitchen, he greeted me with an accented "Good morning, teacher." All smiles he invited me over beside him. Several pages of his magazine were covered with photos of women advertising themselves to prospective husbands.

"Which one do you like, tanito?" he inquired. Almost at random I pointed to one. A long period of study and examination followed, discussing the pros and cons of my choice. As he meant this to be a serious business, I became much amused. I left him for a few minutes to snatch a few bites of breakfast.

"How about this one?" as he hopped over to me. My mouth full of toast, I assented with a nod. In ecstasy he slammed the book to his breast, and then released it with "O she's a swell girl!"

The little man left the house with an air of satisfaction. I learned that he was called Poppy in the settlement, but no one seemed to know his real name. He was a bachelor.

The next Saturday he came along again, this time with a honey pail. He was on his way to Blueberry Rock and wondered if I would accompany him. I found a ten-pound lard pail. Poppy and I set out through a marshy bush of wiry undergrowth and fallen trees. Our way was obstructed now and then by moss-covered boulders. A heap of boulders indicated to us that we were about to ascend Blueberry Rock. Saskatoons, patches of moss and blueberry sprigs blanketed the ridge with a straggling mass of foliage. Yawning caves and gaping crevices made splendid dens for bears and skunks. At the end of one hour of berry-picking we had drifted apart and lost sight of each other. I thought it was high time to round-up my partner. I climbed to the summit of the ridge, and peering down the steep sides saw Poppy kneeling by a boulder, his face buried in his arms. His pail was half full of blueberries. Scuttling rocks came tumbling after me as I hurried down to investigate his trouble.

"What is it?" I said.

He looked up at me with a ghastly face. "Is it gone?" he whispered.

"What gone?" I asked.

"A mamma bear!" he jittered. "I not only plays dead but I feel dead."

My heart thumped as I looked about and saw suspicious-looking caves and openings partially hidden by the overhanging drapery of bushes and vines. We knew now that we had intruded upon a bear's feeding patch. "Come on!" I said in a raised whisper. It wasn't a moment until four weak legs were carrying two frenzied berry-pickers through the swamp at a nightmare pace and daring not to look back at the Sodom behind us.

Strength began to pulsate through our veins when the roof of the school came into view. We heaved a sigh of relief.

"Let's sit down!" Poppy panted.

No sooner had we seated ourselves on a log than he drew from his jacket his much worshipped magazine of feminine portraits. At this sudden composure of mind, the fact that we were without our blueberries caught me by surprise.

"Where are the blueberries?" I interrupted. Possibly Mrs. Bruin was smacking her lips at this very moment over our prized picking. "Let them stay there," we decided.

Ma and Pa saw the funny side of our adventure that night, but both being of a sympathetic nature felt exceedingly sorry for Poppy for losing his berries. They told me that all he ever ate at home was small hard biscuits that he baked himself — no fresh food. His pasty complexion betrayed his faulty diet well enough. But what visions the man had of marrying remained a question, for he made several subsequent visits with his magazine of heroines, then suddenly ceased his appearances.

Then one day we heard some strange news.

Episode VI

Winter Residence and Summer Cottage

One mile in from the gravel on the south side of the clay road lies a low, flat-roofed stable, with a sprawly appearance. None of its four sides is parallel with the road. The north-east side contains a small doorway. Though askew with the road, it is in a harmonizing position with a rivulet flowing along its south-west side. The brink of the brook is furred with pussy willows. The stable is banked on all sides with manure heaped nearly to the roof for protection against the winter winds. Inside this log stable lives a team of horses. The horses are healthy and well cared for. Though absolutely protected from frost in the winter, spring floods swell the rivulet into a torrent. The land around the stable is transformed into a bog until July. Strange about this stable is a makeshift chimney poking out of the roof. Besides a team of horses using this building, it is the "home sweet home" of Poppy. A manger of hay is his bed. In one corner of the shanty is a cookstove in which Poppy bakes his hard biscuits. The shallow windows allow only the rising and setting suns to throw their horizontal beams across the room and flood it with sunlight. Noonday is dull. The thump of a horse's hoof or the munching of hay are the only sounds which pervade the stillness.

But what happens in the spring and summer when boggy ground makes this stable uninhabitable for either man or beast? Across the road is a shelter for the horses, like a colossal table. The horses are exposed to weather on all sides, but protected overhead from the direct rays of the sun by a flat roof. Farther in from the road the land rises to a sharp mound. There is a three-foot square hole in the side of the mound, and a piece of stove pipe on the top. This is Poppy's summer home.

When I first saw this my thoughts reverted to the cave dwellers of Europe. I was awe-stricken for a moment. This was Poppy's summer cottage!

Three months after the Blueberry Rock episode Poppy was on the operating table in Cochrane hospital with a ruined stomach. He died under the anaesthetic. Investigations revealed that he had a wife and three children in Hungary and fifteen thousand dollars besides. The community received the news as a shock. Poppy, though a congenial type of man, was a mysterious character.

POPPY'S SUMMER HOME

Episode VII

A Blue Monday

A crisp, cold January morning with a glittering sun set in a crystal sky made extra fuelling a positive necessity. However, the school soon warmed up owing to the absence of wind. The morning session over, I donned my overcoat, cap and galoshes, and stepped out into the forty-below-zero snap. Hunger pains gnawed and saliva flowed as I thought of my dinner.

A young twenty-one-year-old chap was piling pulpwood on the road near the school. He asked if he could go into the school for a drink. I knew him to be a decent and polite young man and consented. Furthermore, I told him to ask one of the boys to get more water if the pail were empty.

As I entered the kitchen, Ma informed me that my nose was frozen. After the thawing process was over, I sat down to a bowl of simmering hot macaroni soup. The outside door burst open and a voice screamed, "A fire! A fire!"

I dashed into the frosty air with the messenger at my heels, wailing in tones of terror. I could see no smoke around the school, and this consolation assured me that I might yet save the school. But where were the children? Not one could be seen. "Have they not got enough sense to get out when there is a fire?" I asked myself. Perhaps they were salvaging books and clothes. But still there was no sign of belongings in the school yard. "Keep calm!" I repeated to myself as I approached the open doorway.

In eager excitement I beheld a scene that I could not understand. Two young men stood just inside the door with black eyes and blood streaming down their faces, and blood-soaked hair matted to their foreheads. Both of them stood staring at me and panting labouriously. The room was filled with the bawling of frightened school children who stood a safe distance away from the wrestling bout, wringing their hands in a state of frenzy.

"What's this all about?" I quietly asked.

Each apologetically recounted like stories. There had been a little jealousy over a sixteen-year-old girl at the frolic the Sunday night before. The young man whom I permitted to come in for a drink tried to take her handkerchief. Bill, a favourite pupil of mine, attempted to bar him from it and a fight ensued. I liked both the boys, but I made it plain to the young woodman that he had better not come around the school again unless I were there. He said he felt sorry for causing the disturbance. Only a real man can make a confession in front of twenty-five children.

When he left, I called school, and settled the children down to a literature lesson. I thought this would be a good antidote for upset nerves. In the meantime Bill apologized.

The school door opened and Ma set my clothes and galoshes inside. She looked around for a moment, then glaring at Bill she admonished him in her own language, "Shame on you!" Bill hung his head and covered his face while the big sixteen-year-old frame shook in sobs of real shame indeed.

BIG BILL, MY FRIEND, LEFT   BILL'S ASSAILANT, RIGHT

Episode VIII

The French Lesson

"Come over for supper to-night, teacher!" called a voice from the Ellement house as I was passing on my way home after four one afternoon. I went over to the house with my arms laden with books before I made any response. The French grass-widow was eating a fish pie as she stood outside her door awaiting a reply. I told her I should be glad to come back for supper. After depositing my books and capturing a few moments for a snooze at Ma's, I returned to the French home.

A layer of cedar logs served as a floor in this house. Half-grown chickens were running around inside the single room. A few were squatted under the stove. The mud walls and log roof were not whitewashed as at Ma's, but were coated with a thin film of smoke casting a gloom over the room. Supper consisted of fish pie and milk. Conversation was sparing and I felt as though a foreboding evil awaited me. Glaring, black eyes cast hard looks at me quite often.

When the meal was over, Mme. Ellement stood poised over my chair and poured forth a volley of oaths such as I have never heard from a woman.

"You no make my boy bapteest! You no make my boy bapteest!" she screached. Her habit of shouting had developed a chronic gruffness not unlike a man's voice. I had been reading the Scriptures daily in school and was teaching Bible memory work. As I had had difficulty with the Elle-ment boys over their memory work I surmised at this moment that the root of the difficulty lay in the mother. I arose from my chair and stood a safe distance away until the little spitfire came to a stop. I explained to her the regulations regarding religious exercises. Some days later I showed her the first pages of the daily register which contained these regulations.

This mother and her three boys were the only French residents in the section. Besides being of a different faith, their language was also different, thus making the boys distinct from the majority of the pupils who were Hungarian. The mother thought because of this distinction that I had not placed as much emphasis on their education as I did on the rest of the school — a needless suspicion.

Friction between her and me increased. One day I concocted a plan that might remove this friction. As she was a woman who liked to exhibit authority (and we have one in every school section), I thought that if she could come over to the school and help in one of the French lessons that my problem would be solved. I thought, too, that it would possibly motivate the work of my Fifth Class boys to have French taught first hand.

French period was first thing after dinner and Mme. Ellement was to be there for the lesson. I asked her to give them some vocabulary drill, for I wanted to hear the native pronunciation of the words myself. She read a list of French words and the boys were to write the English forms. Then she read a few English expressions which were to be written in French.

I was greatly amused at her pompous and authoritative manner, and the children appeared to get a kick out of it too. She strutted up and down the aisles rapping the knuckles of the pupils with a twelve-inch ruler causing much merriment which would have liked to express itself in an uproar of laughter. Had the taps been severe, antagonism would have arisen in the blood of the pupils. But these feather taps coupled with the woman's authoritative air were highly enjoyed by all of us, even to the assistant herself.

I thanked her for coming. But I realized that a return visit would be of no help to any of us. As she was leaving she said she would be back again. O, me! What a change! But I figured that it was a change for the worse. Her attitude toward me was completely reversed, and too much so. How was I going to tell her I didn't want her again and still retain the amiable feelings which I had tried to foster? I concluded that I had jumped from the frying pan into the fire, and that the French lesson contained something of the ridiculous as well as the sublime.

FRENCH TEACHER AND ESCORT

Episode IX

Storm

February is usually a month of severe winter weather in Northern Ontario.

One day stands out among all others for having been deathly cold. A forty-mile gale was blowing, and the air was filled with sifting snow as I made my way to school that morning. The brave little lad whose mother cared for the school had a fire going in the rusty heater. He was standing over the fire rubbing warmth into his numb fingers when I entered. The school had warmed up a little, but the thermometer still registered twenty below zero. During the winter months the pupils used to put their ink bottles under the stove, so that they would thaw out first thing in the mornings. One of the bottles had burst with the pressure of the freezing process.

I arranged the portable desks around the heater. Extra provision for warmth must be made for anyone attempting to make the trip to school on a day like this.

Before long pupils began to show up, and at nine only three were absent of the twenty-five enrolled. Both dogs and pupils assembled around the stove for a day in school. This was a common occurrence. As many as ten dogs had befriended one another around the heater one other stormy day. But what of the three children who were absent? Had they started out and given up in sheer exhaustion, or were they kept at home?

My fingers became useless for doing much blackboard work.

BILL BALOG, HEAD TURNED

Though I had taught these bush children a little of the etiquette of modern and civilized society, we threw all etiquette aside, and kept our caps and coats on. This reminded me of the time I took young Bill Balog to Cochrane. He had blood poisoning in his hand. Off came his hat when we went into the bank. Again off it came when we entered the Dominion Store. These acts exposed a weakness in my teaching of etiquette. I had not made it clear that it is not necessary to remove the hat in public places such as stores, post offices and such.

We had an interesting day indoors while the snow piled up in little drifts along the inside walls of the school. Toward the middle of the afternoon the storm abated somewhat. I would feel guilty sending the children home early without giving them a maximum amount of teaching for their effort in coming out, yet they had a long trip home over blocked roads, and it would get dark early, I let them go at three thirty.

When I went home, there wasn't a snowflake in the air. The storm passed. As I was sweeping the snow off my feet at Ma's, I noticed that the mercury in the thermometer had vanished out of sight. Papers later indicated that the temperature had fallen to sixty below zero that night.

The fire felt good as Pa kept throwing on tamarack blocks. He told us that during the last winter a neighbour had been frozen to death in the ditch just outside the house. Pa said that during the same winter, one family living two miles beyond the school was ill-clad and ill-fed. The father's affections were in his booze. The children were mere skeletons, and one boy perished from malnutrition. The body of the boy was left in the woodshed till the spring, when the ground would be thoroughly thawed. There were no funeral rites.

It was in a blizzard like this that Ma lost her sense of direction one night when she went over to the neighbour's for some bread.

I went outside to view the stars and take one last look at the thermometer before going to bed. Pa slipped a stocking over his head as he puffed out the light, chuckling something to himself, while his massive frame shook — the outward expression of a good-natured spirit.

TIN STOVE PLUS RESTING PLACE FOR SLED DOGS

Episode X

Used Rubber

The warm April sun began to soften the snow and thus the children found two new sports, snowballing and making snowmen. A school with such a wide range of ages as I had, is a disciplinary problem from the standpoint of protecting the younger tots from the abuse and rough play of those possessed with more mature strength and weight. The snowballing became no longer a sport, but a one-sided melee where ruffians and bullies pelted little children mercilessly. It was necessary for me to intervene, and I made the rule, and emphasized the consequences should the rule be broken, that there was to be no snowballing unless even sides were chosen, and that no one must be forced to participate if he or she did not care to.

Not many weeks after this ruling was made, a sleighload of hay drove through the schoolyard. Frank Agoston, a pupil who had recently finished school, was driving the team. He made a good bait for a snowballing and one of the boys let fire with the result that four or five others followed suit.

I realized that this was not an affair demanding corporal punishment, yet I must not go back on my word. At noon, when all had assembled in their seats, I asked for a show of hands of those who were throwing the snowballs. One boy failed to raise his hand and I waited for a short moment. Meanwhile, it dawned upon me that if I punished the rest it might show up the remaining little culprit. I knew who it was all this time, but I do like a boy to own up to a thing even if he has to be forced by circumstances into doing so. I proceeded with my painful duty and nothing made me feel more cheap than the strapping of my friend, Bill Balint, who towered over me like Gulliver over a Lilliputian. He had become a close companion of mine and was almost my age. But no matter how humiliating the job, it must be performed.

The desired result was obtained, and the one boy who was slow to submit rose to his feet. He was a twelve-year-old chap, small, wiry, and possessed with a stubborn streak, the which I expected would expose its rawness at this time. In order to test it I handed him my jack-knife and asked him to cut a gad from the bushes outside the door. If he passed the test, I would not punish him.

Lo and behold, he came in, handed me the rod of correction and stood there waiting for its application. He had passed the test. I must not use it. After brief counselling I asked him to write four lines from the reader a number of times:

"You never know, you cannot tell
What harm a little lie may do;
There's just one way that's safe and sure,
And that is just be always true."

The satisfied looks of a number of the children showed that his deserts had been justly meted out, while other tense individuals relaxed with a sigh of relief. Though if I had the same problem to solve to-day I should not follow the above course of procedure. What would you do?

FRANK AGOSTON

Episode XI

Assessor

I received a letter from my inspector one day which read: "Would you favour me by undertaking the job of assessing the properties on the next concession south of yours? Gauge them from forty to sixty dollars apiece according to the type of dwelling. Give names of all those living on each property, and the occupation of every person over twenty-one years of age. Please let me know soon if you can undertake this. I aim to open up a new school section."

This was a command put in the form of a request. A dutiful teacher must go ahead with it whether he liked it or not, and as I was always looking for adventure I seized up on the idea without reluctance.

The next morning, Saturday, I was hopping along dead branches and making raids for rotten stumps as the May sun tried its best to dry up the tons of surface water lying in uncertain depths in the brushland around me. Even though my feet were drenched to the ankles, I still took strenuous precautions to seek dry footing, which might mean a flea-hop or the bound of a wood hare. The absurdity of taking such pains, with my feet already wet, never struck me till I had reached dry road.

A sickening odour filled the air as I stepped up to the door of my first hut. There were five men seated around a table with partly-filled glasses of home-brew. The housewife was stirring more in a boiler on the stove.

"Come in! Come in! entreated a droll voice from the table. The empty, sleepy looks of drunken men turned my way.

Mouths were gaping terrifyingly. The floor was carpeted with a film of evaporated tobacco juice, a mahogany brown.

I explained my mission and proceeded to ask questions, but I could not ascertain who was the owner of the hut. The men were too intoxicated to think or speak clearly, and the housewife knew only a smattering of English. I discovered that she was Czecho-Slovakian, but her indignation was aroused when I asked her her occupation. In fact, few questions were necessary as one could size up the situation quite easily with a few glances and a sniff of the air. I planked down a fifty for the assessment, as I decided it was an average dwelling.

A friendly couple with a well-trained family of children lived across the road. The log hut was substantially built and quite roomy inside. There was a single room with a bed in each of three corners, a stove in the fourth corner and a table in the centre. The little Czech mother was rolling out some homemade macaroni on the bare table-top. As I was leaving, the young Czech invited me to come back for supper and to remain all night if necessary. I thanked him and accepted his twofold invitation, as I already felt the effects of the tramp through the swamp, and knew I would be dead-beat if I endeavoured to make a home trip that night. Furthermore, I did not relish the idea of striking out at dusk to step blindly in a hit-and-miss style through swamp, should the night darken early. To become one of the family, and eat and sleep in the same room was a parallel experience with my first night at Driftwood.

There was only one other house worth mentioning. The family was Hungarian and the house was putrid and smelly. Cobwebs curtained the windows, and dirty dishes lay in a disorderly fashion on the table. It was a noted bawdy old den. A worthless scoundrel of a human being lay useless on a couch. A gentle-dispositioned woman invited me inside and I immediately sized her up as a wolf in sheep's clothing. They insisted that I take a cup of milk. Only to oblige them I did so. For how many days back that cup never saw soap or water I dare not guess, but it was stained with tea and dirty mouths. Perhaps their black cat knew more about washing dishes than they did.

Two weeks later I was horrified in finding a large, hollow ulcer just inside my lower lip. The remembrance of this place of vice drove me into severe mental anguish, for I thought I had contracted a venereal disease; and here I was seventeen miles from a doctor. But the ulcer disappeared in a few days.

Sunday morning dawned bright and hot in the little Czech colony. The air was motionless, and visible waves of heated air playing over tar-paper roofs foretold a suffocating afternoon. On the edge of the swamp a colony of garter snakes lay basking in the sunshine. Further on, frogs, startled by the rare sounds of footsteps, splashed into the puddles of warm water, unaware of the nearness of their reptilian enemies. Stonco's house was the first sign that the settlement was not far away. And I was glad to plant my feet on terra firma once again.

Episode XII

A Caller

Returning from a visit across the road one 1937 September Saturday, I beheld Ma and Pa engaged in a wrestling match. Ma had just finished patching up the walls with pig manure, and Pa had not yet begun to apply the whitewash, when this good-natured tussle began. Ma had Pa down on his back near the manure pail when I entered. The room was stinking like a pigsty. As soon as they saw me the fun had to stop. Ma gazed out of the window and studied a plodding figure coming down the road, yet half a mile away.

"What's that?" she whispered in an air of suspicion.

"The relief inspector!" supplied Pa.

Never did I see Ma and Pa flit about the house as I did that moment. Money was hidden among the log rafters in the ceiling. Sweeping, dusting, and placing were done in rapid succession. Good clothes disappeared. I was warned to inform the inspector that there was no money in the house, if I were asked to tell him anything. I was supposed to tell him that I was paying twenty dollars a month for board instead of thirty. My respect for this couple was lowered as never before. I hoped that the inspector would not say a word to me, as I did not want to betray either party. At first I had an inclination to hide. However, I made up my mind that I would face the music and tell the truth if I had to say anything at all.

There was a gentle tap at the door and a blond, middle-aged man of medium build put in appearance. He was dressed in a plain, dark brown suit, and carried a large black case.

A crank handle projecting from the side exhibited the fact that it was a portable phonograph. I realized that no relief inspector ever carried a phonograph, and I heaved a deep sigh of relief as he opened the instrument. The visitor sniffed the manure-scented air, casting significant glances around the room. Apparently he was a Judge Rutherford agent. I knew some Hungarian but I could not make head or tail out of the lecture played on the phonograph. Ma and Pa listened with quiet interest.

The agent displayed Hungarian literature for sale, exhorting and making low offers in order to sell his propaganda. If he was an angel of light I was a demon of the underworld, for I opposed everything that he did.

Fortunately, I knew enough of the language to tell my friends that these books were twenty per cent good and eighty per cent false. At this they produced stacks of literature from their trunks which vendors had left on their calls through the settlement. No doubt the community was full of it. As I believed that Ma and Pa were being duped into accepting a faith which, I believed, was not sound, I intervened and explained that they needed no more books, as they were daily readers of the Bible itself. Many evenings had been spent in discussing various Bible chapters. While they read from a Hungarian Bible, I would read the corresponding chapter in the English version. As they had taken a new interest in Bible reading, I hated to see this propaganda invading their belief.

The agent quickly gathered his books and records together slipping out of the door to visit more patrons, or, better still, victims.

As our neighbour, the French mistress, loathed the duty of entertaining strangers, she slyly donned her hat and coat when she saw prospects of an intended visit. She met the agent on her way over to our place and nodded him a good-day. The poor woman led an irreputable life, and as she fingered an Eaton's catalogue at the table, a few bed bugs dropped from her coat amongst the leaves of the book. In a few moments she returned home satisfied that her intended visitor had gone on.

Paper for kindling lasted a long time that fall as Judge Rutherford's books fell prey to the consuming flames of the cookstove.

Ma and Pa finished their whitewashing which cleared the air of its tainted smell, but Pa refused Ma's challenge for another wrestling bout.

OUTDOOR OVEN AND WONDER BREAD

Episode XIII

A Medical Interlude

In January 1938 I took up residence in the teacherage at the school which had just been built the fall before. A bachelor career began. My evenings were comparatively quiet, but I spent a good deal of my time reading and visiting.

The teacherage was a light shack and anything but weatherproof. The contractors evidently aimed at ample provision for ventilation. What's more, the unseasoned lumber, lining the shack began a shrinking process which was the result of a band of whistling woodwinds. I packed copies of the Owen Sound Daily Sun Times into these cracks. Even during the warm weather in the spring the cracks around the door had to be packed to keep out the mosquitoes.

Every morning at three o'clock the fire had to be refuelled. Occasionally, I overslept the hour and the fire died out, whereupon I would crawl back into bed till daylight. Quite often I had risen early in the morning craving a warm breakfast but finding my bread frozen as hard as a piece of India rubber.

Among my mail collection one Saturday morning in April, I found a letter from the Medical Officer of Health notifying me of a toxoid clinic to be held in the school a week from the following Monday.

The week was spent in writing out notices to parents in all parts of the section, and to many beyond the section in unorganized territory. Some of the notices were written in English, others were penned in Hungarian and Czecho-Slovakian.

TEACHERAGE APPENDED TO SCHOOL

The doctor, with his wife who was a graduate nurse, was scheduled to be at the school some time before four o'clock Monday afternoon. Some young children came with their brothers and sisters in the morning. Others were carried miles through swamp, bush or trail in the afternoon. Wagons brought families from greater distances, and soon the schoolyard was a scene similar to an old-fashioned garden party.

A group of children played ball. Men sat in clusters talking and smoking. The women and the small children occupied a different corner of the yard, while both sexes of young people mingled together, jesting and joking with one another.

Anxious eyes viewed the long stretch of clay road as any one of the approaching wagons might be the one which was hired by the doctor and his wife. Imagine the muteness of the crowd standing in awe as the doctor in a neatly tailored dark suit, accompanied by a full-uniformed nurse stepped down from the wagon, while the people themselves appeared in peasant attire. Even the babies seemed to be less noisy than usual as the notable spectacles entered the doorway with their satchels in hand.

The doctor requested that the school children be given the treatment first. The windows were thrust open to extremity, and in a few minutes the children had received their doses. An English exercise awaited them on the blackboard while mothers lined the aisles with smaller children. One mother with three children had stumbled through three miles of thick swamp growth with a baby in her arms, and another two toddling after her. No provision was made should the

DOOR LEADING TO TEACHERAGE

weather change for the worse. Most of the little folk took the needle with a smile. A few led out in a lively howl. My children were exceptionally well-behaved and well-mannered that day. Some gave their seats to mothers standing in line and they rendered this kindness without any confusion whatsoever. If that was the effect visitors had on my class I was wishing they would come more often.

This was the first of a series of toxoid treatments, and the response of the people was gratifying to the extent that it was pathetic, as distance and lack of transportation or bad weather made no difference to them in their determination to do the utmost regarding the health of their children. Most of those who took the first treatment received certificates for the completion of the whole series of treatments.

One Saturday an unexpected and friendly visit was paid me by the doctor and his wife. No words of encouragement are more keenly felt in my memory than the words the doctor spoke on leaving, "Keep up the good work. You're doing a good job back here." Thank you, Dr. Brunet.

SOUTH SIDE OF SCHOOL

Episode XIV

Laura Secord

Quite lamb-like, March 1938 was sliding into the past. Quite lamb-like, I closed my register, addressed my monthly report to the inspector and tidied my table: this spelling book belongs here on the table. "Robinson Crusoe" goes on the shelf. The shelf does not appear to be as full as it should be. Some books are misplaced. Some are really missing! I return to my table. Where is my French dictionary? That old pocket watch that my brother let me have has disappeared. My pulse quickens. No use getting in a stew. Sit down and think about it. When did I see those things last? Yesterday and to-day I had made constant use of the old watch. It was keeping perfect time with my wrist watch this afternoon. April the first? Not yet. The children have not made a mistake in the date? No. Have I? Let me see. This is Thursday the thirty-first of March 1938. Right! Maybe I'm getting rattled.

March was going out like a lamb, but for me that lamb was in a state of metamorphosis, half lamb and half lion. The playful little wag of a fleecy tail began to swing and lash like the ropy tail of a lion.

Thump! Thump! The door rattled, and in walked Leon, the youngest brother of the four French boys. The eldest one, Jacques, seventeen, had just returned to the settlement from serving two sentences in jail. The third, John, had dropped out of school — epilepsy. Robert was still in school but not very trustworthy. Leon, eleven, was quite honest but had the spicy French temperament which sometimes broke through the surface of his meek spirit.

In his high voice: "Did you miss anything from the school?" He unravelled the maze of mystery completely. His eldest brother had commissioned Robert to get as many things from the school as he thought he could smuggle away without causing any noticeable vacancy. Some of the books they were going to sell.

I took the night to think about it.

The next day Robert did not come to school, as he knew that Leon had betrayed them in exposing their mischief to me.

Friday passed as usual, but subconsciously throughout the day I had conceived several methods of approaching the boys and devised certain courses of punishment. But to make the proper selections was a terrific problem. School had been dismissed an hour when a black figure dashed past the windows and bounded through the open doorway. It halted within three feet of my table.

A high voice said: "Mr. Leonard, I heard my eldest brother say he was coming down to your place to-night with his hunting knife." I did not relish the thought of sleeping in the teacherage that night. I had never locked my door nights and never had cause to fear anyone in the settlement, as we all seemed to be one big family, each in his own particular way trying to help the rest of the community.

However, I must admit that now a cowardly fear gripped me which forced me into making plans to lock up here or sleep at the Rokus house for the night. After supper I decided on the latter plan.

The next day was Saturday which I spent visiting, or more correctly, bumming. As I lay on my couch that night, the recent excitement restrained the sedative effects of the Northern air, and I could not sleep. Could I count sheep? I did not want to. I could not, even if I had tried. All I could mumble to myself was coward, bum, coward, bum, coward . . . bum . . . coward. . . .

I read all day Sunday.

Monday at nine o'clock Robert was the only absentee. And again after four o'clock Leon returned with more news. John and Robert had left home to catch a freight train, and the mother wanted me there to write a letter to be forwarded to police headquarters explaining our predicament. I was glad for the opportunity to talk things over with the mother, but thought it unadvisable to report it yet. However, the mother and a neighbour man who was in on the discussion thought we had better write while we had a chance, but that chance did not come. Just then the two forms of the boys passed the window and entered the door behind my back. Each was carrying a pile of new shirts, not yet out of their cellophane wrappings, and retreated into the bedroom to relieve themselves of their loot. While they were there, the neighbour visitor catapulted out the door and disappeared across the clearing. The mother, seated at the opposite side of the table from me, had a complete view of the boys as they entered. She motioned wild-eyed to me that one of them had a knife projecting from his sleeve. The knives and forks which were already on the supper table she quickly seized and hid under the tablecloth.

I managed to keep up a "friendly" conversation with the boys for fifteen minutes, then decided I had better go home.

On Friday Leon came to me with the report that the eldest boy had run at his mother with his knife poised above her when two of the brothers intercepted. This was the last straw. The quickest and safest way out of this mess was to telephone Cochrane headquarters at once. The fire-ranger had a telephone, but this meant I had to pass in full view of the French home. I took my packsack along ostensibly on personal business but still exposed to the suspicions of the would-be criminals. This packsack business reminded me of Laura Secord and her cow.

Two officers showed up in an hour's time. The boys had cached the library books in a box in the bush. After a short trial the eldest boy was sent to a reform school and the brother was put on a year's probation. The last I heard of the eldest boy he was working on a fruit farm in Niagara and is entirely reformed, not only reformed but has been converted by mission workers and is now leading a beautiful Christian life.

MA

Episode XV

Disgraced

The Hungarian language is full of hard-sounding con-
sonants, which gives it a staccato effect. English in contrast is
liquid and quiet. For example, note the difference between
"eleg" and its English equivalent, "enough." This example is
typical of the whole language. Hungarians also put much
more vigour into their enunciation than we do. Their speech
has such carrying power that one can stand on the doorstep
of a settlement home and shout a message to his next-door
neighbour. Their system of phonics is simple. The single
sounds and their combinations unchangingly keep the one
pronunciation, whereas the English varies. Our word "read"
is subject to two pronunciations. "Wr," "ur," "er," "ir," "r"
have the same pronunciations. The Hungarian has only one
letter to express that sound.

In school I used the Budapest high school text book of
English grammar. I also hektographed dozens of labelled
diagrams for English word study.

I had a keen interest in the Hungarian language and tried
to make practical use of it as much as I could. I had often
said, "Koszonom" (thank you) at the table. But one day
something was passed to me, and, in refusing, I thought I
was saying, "No, thank you." I put "nem" (no) and
"koszonom" (thank you) together. But this makes a
ridiculous combination. Literally, "Nem Koszonom" means
"I don't thank you." I was corrected immediately and
graciously by Ma who was not in the least insulted.

On another occasion I used an expression in the presence
of Ma and Pa which I had used numerously during my visits

throughout the section. Pa reprimanded me in a ferociously disgusting tone of voice. He knew the English interpretation, but hesitated to say it when I asked him. Finally, he mumbled, "_____." The expression was of such a vulgar nature that I have never seen its English version in print, nor should I ever expect to. My humiliation and disgrace were so overwhelming that I craved a pile of desert sand in which to bury my head, and an ostrich for company. I saw in my visions that night, as I lay in bed the ostrich and myself, side by side, head buried, one labelled "fear" and the other "shame."

The next day I was to visit Balog's for dinner. How could I? But I did. They had often heard me abusing the Hungarian language. They had sweetened macaroni in a huge dishpan set in the centre of the table. All that were hungry, and the one that was not, gathered around with forks to eat out of the common dish. I stuffed a few bites into a digestive system which strongly protested, while chickens, fluttering about the room, increased the unsanitary conditions of the floor. My previous day's experience had sunk into oblivion for a time at least.

One day I was teaching a Latin vocabulary to my Fifth Class (Grade IX) and upon uttering one of the words in the list all the pupils fixed their eyes upon me in consternation. A few of them were sent into giggles, but I noticed particularly that the well-bred pupils kept a sober look and returned to their work.

I soon learned that the commonest expressions in Hungarian are filthy bywords or swearing, and are the most easily picked up. Likewise, a foreigner does not need to be blamed if swearing is all the English he knows. We are guilty, not they.

PULPWOOD IN THE BUSH

Episode XVI

Bush Fire

One May afternoon after a ponderous lesson in English phonics with my Hungarian pupils I fell asleep at my table with my head on my arm. When I awoke, it was six o'clock and there was a numbness in my arm which remained for two weeks.

No wonder the pupils seemed dazed at the inconsistency of the English language that afternoon, their own mother tongue being comparatively simple. Yet they were alert and quite interested. If one sounds "ough" he will discover that it has various pronunciations. How many sounds has it? Read these words: though, thought, through, rough, trough, bough. How is a pupil of a foreign tongue going to pronounce this group of letters when he sees it? He does not know. He will take a chance on any one of six pronunciations. To memorize a few of its commonest appearances would be a slight help but not a complete solution.

The day had been hot and the air was chokingly saturated with smoke from distant forest and grass fires. As I blew out the lamp that night, that smoke brought several thoughts to my mind. I recalled Mrs. Susanna Moodie's experience trapped in a forest fire and I cowardly hoped that a repetition of that experience would not occur with me. As for the school, I did not worry. I longed to see a permanent weatherproof building erected, and the sooner the better. How the school board secured even a thousand-dollar policy on the building still baffles me. Then I thought of the good work that the fire rangers were doing in Northern Ontario.

This is interesting work. Fire towers cover the whole District of Cochrane for the purpose of locating fires. Each tower is equipped with a circular table on which is marked the three hundred and sixty degrees of the circle. A pointer is fastened to a swivel at the centre of the circle. When a spot of smoke is sighted on the horizon, the pointer is directed toward the smoke and the degree reading on the circumference of the circle over which the tip of the pointer rests is reported to headquarters in the town of Cochrane by telephone, each tower being connected with the others and with head office by a private telephone system.

FIRE TOWER

PEELED WOOD ON ROADSIDE FOR HAULING

Another tower sights the same fire. But the smoke from the second tower will be in a different direction. Thus a different degree finding will be reported.

On the wall in the Cochrane office hangs a large map. All towers in the district are marked with common pins stuck into the map from which hang long, cotton threads. When two towers report a degree finding the free end of the thread of the first tower is grasped in one hand, and the thread is placed at an angle to follow the degree line which was reported. Likewise the thread from the second tower is placed with the other hand in accordance with its degree finding. The two threads cross each other and the point of intersection is the location of the fire. The department knows through records whether or not the owner of that lot has permission to burn slashwood. Immediate investigation is of vital importance to the conservation of Northern Ontario's paper bush.

I slept soundly that night and awakened early next morning to see men standing along the road beside their respective piles of pulpwood doing a lot of wishful thinking, for a strong north wind was bringing clouds of smoke closer to the settlement. I snatched a bit of bologna and then went outside. The settlers would be helpless to save the wood if it caught. Nevertheless, they would have the consolation of being near when their most valued treasure disappeared — just as a person rushes to the bedside of his dying friend though helpless he may be.

I did not stay outside for five minutes. I was set on packing my books and clothes. All that Saturday morning I packed my personal effects, rolled up the mattress, folded up the cot, put the library books into boxes and placed everything at the door ready to be hauled away if need be.

HAULING PULPWOOD

74

There was bush on the north, east and south sides of the school. By midafternoon all this bush was burning. Large spruces sent puffs of thick, black smoke into the air, while underbrush and dry timber fed clouds of gray smoke. The wind had died down and the green, spring grass in the schoolyard acted as a check to creeping flames of fire. The school was safe thus far and the wood was not touched. We were hoping and praying that the night might remain calm, and were faithlessly longing for rain.

When twilight fell a few black fingers silhouetted against the sky was all that remained of the surrounding bush. Tongues of flame still licked the sides of a few stubborn trunks, while red coals on the forest floor lay imbedded in other resisting matter.

I was tired, but I dared not sleep. Through the night the stillness was punctuated with pistol-shot reports as trunks of green spruces toppled over to become part of a bed of ruins.

Sunday was rest day.

The owner upon whose lot the fire had its beginning paid heavy fines as he was burning without a permit.

PULPWOOD AND SCHOOL

HAULING PULPWOOD
COMMUNIST ORGANIZER ON RIGHT

RANGER IN HIS TOWER

Episode XVII

Humiliation to the Nth Degree

One spring night (I cannot place the date) while I was at Ma's, both Ma and Pa went to a party. They left me home with the mosquitoes. A pail of smouldering chips outside the screen door guarded the entrance against the invading pests. When Ma and Pa were leaving I assured them that everything would be all right. Despite their efforts to keep out mosquitoes my room was whining with the brutes. So I devised a scheme that brought shame and repentance and sorrow.

I had several sulphur candles which I had purchased in Cochrane with a view to some day trying them out on the mosquitoes. I thought that this was a good time to try out my fumigation experiment.

The result proved a failure in more ways than one. Every mosquito remained alive and seemed more vivacious than before, and all Ma's many and beautiful house plants folded up their leaves and died. What I must do for restitution provided a greater problem than the mosquito one itself. By this time, I am sure, the Hungarians were itching to run me out of the settlement and I would not have blamed them a bit.

BLACK AND WHITE PAINTING
3 FT BY 2 FT BY GRADE 6 PUPILS

Episode XVIII

Boldi

Every night at eleven o'clock during the spring of 1938 a young man by name of Boldi passed through the school grounds singing or whistling with an apparent levity of spirit. He was on his way home from a hard day's work in a neighbour's bush, heartened for the moment by a pint or two of beer. He was well educated and normally happy but took occasional despondent fits, and was persistently annoyed with the gout.

I awoke one morning from a successful rest to find the room filled with radiant May sunshine. Breakfast consisted of my regular portion of white bread and bologna. How refreshing it was to stand at the schoolhouse door and view a landscape bathed in warm sunlight, to hear a multitude of bird voices, and sense the balmy odour of bursting willow buds! Yesterday had been a wet day which added to the weariness of a six-mile tramp to Driftwood for mail. To-day was Sunday, which found me with no clean underwear for the coming week. I kindled a fire in the box stove, heated a pailful of water and went to work with my washing equipment arrayed in the school yard. This duty completed I went into the school to read. Unexpectedly the door opened and one of my pupils stumbled in, breathless, and stuttering excitedly! "B-b-b-b-oldi hanged himself!" I looked at him in eager excitement waiting for the details.

"Kovacs woke up this morning and no Boldi could he find. He went out to the stable. When he opened the door there was Boldi's dead body swinging in the doorway. Kovacs was so scared he ran back into his house and locked the door.

Then he came to tell us. Dad has gone to ring Cochrane police." With that he skipped out the door to carry the news to the rest of the settlement.

Boldi and Kovacs dwelt in a single-roomed hut two miles back behind the school in tangled swamp and bushland. Two hours later, when I was at the pump, a team and wagon with two officers passed by. I was invited to go along and "join the fun," and as I was always seeking adventure I grabbed my mosquito veil and managed to catch up to them by the time the wagon came to its stopping place. Those with rubber boots walked on, but the remainder of the crowd stayed with the wagon. In a short interval of time the two husky officers with laborious strides arrived with the corpse tied to a pole an end of which rested on a shoulder of each officer. The crowd had grown to great proportions by now, and as the procession moved down the long stretch of clay road, peasant women came running out of their houses to have a peep at the suicide. One woman unwrapped some of the sacking around his head and laughed in the dead man's face. These realities were too much for me. I returned to the school to resume my reading.

COMMUNIST SCHOOL BOARD

"WORMS" PATIENT LEFT

Episode XIX

Haircut and Worms

A month after the suicide I received an interesting letter from home, interesting because we had arranged to time the sunset on June twenty-first. In Owen Sound the sun disappeared at eight o'clock. At Driftwood its disc dropped behind the horizon at eight twenty-two. Both observations were made on level country. This proves that the farther one goes north in the summer the longer become the days.

After I had devoured my mail packet to the last word I took a stroll down the sunbaked road, a perfect floor of solid clay. The road in this state attracts strollers old and young alike, but particularly those of a romantic age. What better amusement could a young man find than to serenade his lady on this lover's lane in the quiet evening under a spring moon. An accompaniment of wakening frog voices would sweeten the strains of his Hungarian lovelilt. The road not only served its purpose in leisure hours but it also was a by-way for pulpwood trucks during work days.

Who is responsible for such road conditions? No one seems to recognize or appreciate his work. He is a little old Irishman of about seventy years of age, has had at least a dozen children. He is a small hard-working man grown infirm and weak and palsy-shaken. But still he is faithful in this road duties. His last grading had put the road into its present fitness. He was unmistakably a master potter at road making. Clay roads have to be attended to immediately after a rain while they are yet pliable. During the busy season this road received faithful attention . . . and now I was making use of it. I thought I would visit a few of the neighbours. I would call on Rokus first, the community barber.

He had no set rates. Customers paid as much or as little as they felt so disposed. He was a happy man now, as his family had arrived recently from Hungary to begin pioneering together in new lands of Ontario. Theresa was a girl of twelve; Peter, a boy of fifteen — both pupils of mine. It so happened that I had met this family in Union Station the previous Christmas during their immigration. I had recognized them by their dress, and, using a jumble of Hungarian words and a few flourishes of hands I found out that they were on their way to Driftwood.

As Rokus was pinning the cloth around my neck for a haircut, he asked me for news about the murder.

NEW FAMILY — COMMUNICATION IN HUNGARIAN ONLY

"What murder?" I asked.

He explained that the little Irishman had committed a murder in his own bush that morning. The storekeeper's hired man was ordered to seize wood from the Irishman's bush as his store bills had mounted up considerably and there were no prospects of them being paid. The poor Irishman through desperation and loyalty to his family of thirteen children raised his gun, unhesitatingly pulled the trigger, and a cartridge of shot sank into the hired man's chest.

Public sentiment rose in favour of the Irishman and a petition was circulated begging leniency on behalf of the murderer. He was sent to Haileybury, and that's the last I heard of him.

Mrs. Rokus treated me to some hot fresh buns filled with new cheese. While I was enjoying this delicious repast, Peter rushed into the house howling with pain. He had cut his foot chopping wood. Mrs. Rokus entreated, "Tanito, tanito, teseg!" — Teacher, teacher, please — Amid blood, sweat and tears I managed to loosen the shoe sufficiently to remove it easily. From my scanty knowledge of physiology I recalled that dark blood flowing smoothly was a sign of a venous break. It was not a bad cut to deal with, but it reminded me of my predecessor and his maternity case.

An uneventful week followed. But the week-end put me in a highly embarrassing position. I was to be interpreter at the doctor's office in Cochrane for a Hungarian woman whose supposed ailment was intestinal worms. The result of the diagnosis, however, turned out to be unexpected and very embarrassing to both of us. As I struggled for the commonest expressions in Hungarian and discovered the position I was in, I wondered that the doctor did not treat me there as a nerve patient. That night I was rewarded with a plate of blueberry preserves and an extra bottle which I was to pack into my trunk and take home with me.

I visited the community hall the next night. Crowded with a banqueting and dancing throng this building is the monthly scene of Sunday-night parties. As I was leaving the table I noticed that the label on my bottle was not ginger ale for which I had taken it to be, but ale of an intoxicating nature. What was to be the benefit of all my hygiene lessons on the harmful effects of alcohol to my pupils when in their midst they should see a hypocrite blithely drinking ale. If I had had a tail I would have gone home with it between my legs.

You will recognize me as a temperance crank but if you have seen what I have seen you will agree that hard drinking does nobody any good. I was reminded of the family that was so steeped in drink that a little boy died of starvation and neglect and his body was left in the woodshed till late spring. He was a frozen corpse for three months. The other members of the family were as thin as rails.

The day that school closed I stood at the door till the last of my pupils had disappeared perhaps forever out of my sight. I knelt at my desk and praised God for these young people and asked His guidance over them to make them into Christian citizens, and I thanked Him for the share I had in shaping their lives.

COMMUNIST CLASS AT COMMUNITY HALL

COMMUNIST CLASS

KEN BALINT TEN YEARS LATER

List of Illustrations

List of Illustrations, cont'd.

Notes

Notes